Part 1

Using Assessn

D0886302

Contents

INTRODUCTION

This Assessment Book includes information about assessment in Macmillan/McGraw-Hill's *Adventures in Time and Place,* directions for administering and scoring Unit Tests and Performance Assessments, blackline masters, and answer keys.

Description of the Assessments

There are two types of assessments provided in this book for *People Together:* Unit Tests and Performance Assessments.

Part 3 has **Unit Test** blackline masters for each unit in People Together. Each Unit Test comprises three sections:

- The **Content** section has 10 test questions, or items, about the content of the unit. Five of the items are multiple-choice questions and five are short-answer questions — fill-in, matching, written response.

- The **Skills** section has 5 short-answer items for each skill taught in the unit.

- The **Writing** section has one essay question measuring the student's knowledge of the content and ability to apply the skills in the unit. The essay question includes a visual stimulus and requires the student to write sentences or a brief paragraph.

Answer Keys for the Unit Tests appear in sequence in Part 2.

Part 4 provides one **Performance Assessment** for each unit in People Together. The Performance Assessment is based on the Unit Project in the Unit Review of the Pupil's Edition. Each Unit Project results in a product that can be assessed. It also involves a process that can be evaluated through observation.

The Performance Assessment for each unit provides guidelines for using the Unit Project assessment. It includes the following:

- A statement of the **goal** of the Unit Project

- **Suggestions** for modeling and instruction that will enable students to complete the project

- **Portfolio Opportunities** that provide suggestions for evaluating student performance—including self-assessment and peer assessment—and incorporating the assessment into a portfolio

- A **Scoring Rubric** designed to help teachers evaluate each student's performance and score it as Excellent, Good, Fair, Poor, or Unscorable

Principles of Assessment

Assessment in *Adventures in Time and Place* involves the use of multiple measures in a wide variety of authentic situations to evaluate what students can do. Information collected through various forms of assessment is used for evaluation or making judgments about student performance. Forms of assessment provided with this program include both paper-and-pencil tests and performance assessments. Our approach to assessment is based on the following principles.

Assessment should be closely integrated with instruction. It should be based on the goals of instruction, and it should measure what is taught, in the way in which it is taught.

Assessment should be based on the notion of progress — evaluating student progress toward achieving the goals and objectives of instruction. It should be based on the ability to apply critical thinking strategies in a variety of contexts, not only on mastering isolated skills.

Assessment should be continuous, throughout the school year, and should incorporate a wide variety of modes and types of assessment. Frequent assessments will provide formative information that is useful in guiding instruction. A wide variety of assessments will provide a comprehensive profile of each student.

Assessment tasks and activities should be direct and authentic, reflecting what students actually need to be able to do. Assessment in authentic situations requires real-life tasks, which may involve any number of activities, from everyday classroom observations to student work samples to independent projects.

Authentic assessment activities should integrate social studies curriculum with all of the language arts: reading, writing, listening, speaking, and viewing. Language arts are integrated in every aspect of real life, and they should be integrated in the classroom.

Assessment should include self-assessment and cooperative efforts between teacher and students, among student peers, and involving parents. Students can learn a great deal from understanding and applying the standards of good work to their own achievements.

The assessments provided with this program are based on these principles of assessment. The Unit Tests and Performance Assessments are intended to be administered at the end of each unit. They are designed to help you determine how well students have mastered the content of the unit and how well they can apply the skills taught in the unit. Other ways of using tests, performance assessments, and portfolios with this program are described on the next page.

Assessment: Questions and Answers

Can the Unit Tests be used in different ways?

Yes. The Unit Tests have three sections: Content, Skills, and Writing. You may choose to give any or all of these sections when you administer the test, and you may use the sections of the test in other ways. For example, you might decide to use the Content section as a test and the Skills and Writing sections for instructional practice or follow-up instruction.

How can I use performance assessments with this program?

There are three general approaches to using performance assessment with this program. First, you can observe students in the classroom—during everyday activities and in specific activities outlined in the Teacher's Edition. Second, you can administer the Performance Assessment for each unit. Third, you can use portfolios.

How do I use the Performance Assessments?

The Performance Assessments are based on the Unit Projects in the Pupil Edition Unit Reviews. When you have completed a unit, use the Performance Assessment guidelines in Part 4 to help prepare students to complete the project and evaluate their performance. Each Performance Assessment offers suggestions for introducing the project and assisting students in its completion, suggestions for using the assessment as a portfolio opportunity, and a scoring rubric for evaluating student performance.

What is portfolio assessment?

Simply stated, a portfolio is an organized collection of a student's work. A portfolio system can be as simple as a set of folders and a box to keep them in, but portfolio assessment is much more than that: it is a powerful concept for developing a comprehensive profile of each student.

How do I get started with portfolios?

Start with something simple and easy to manage. Introduce portfolios to the students as a way to organize their work. Tell them that they will be choosing their best works to put into the portfolio. At the beginning of the year, you may want to model the process by showing them your own portfolio or inviting guests, such as artists or photographers, to come in and show students their portfolios.

How do I involve students in portfolios?

Involving students is a critical part of portfolio assessment. Tell students they are responsible for taking care of their own portfolios. Talk with students to set goals for each unit and for the year. Work with them to choose their best works to help them meet their goals. Have students evaluate their own works by writing notes or completing self-assessments for each work they put into the portfolio. Periodically, have a portfolio review conference with students to look at what they have done, help them assess their own progress, and set new goals for the next unit.

How can I figure out students' grades from these assessment materials?

The Unit Tests are designed to be scored by section, and the score for each section can easily be converted to a percentage score for grading purposes. For the Writing section of the Unit Test and for the Performance Assessments, the student's performance can be scored on a 4-point scale. This type of score can also be converted to a percentage score for grading, as explained in the following pages.

Administering Assessments

The Unit Tests and Performance Assessments are designed to be used with each unit. Before administering these assessments, familiarize yourself with the assessments themselves and the guidelines in this Teacher's Manual.

Administering Unit Tests

The **Unit Tests** in Part 3 are designed for group administration. You may choose to administer the complete Unit Test or any of its parts: Content, Skills, Writing.

These tests are not intended to be timed. Students should be given ample time to complete the tests. However, for planning purposes, the chart below shows the estimated time required to administer each section of the test.

Section	Number of Items	Estimated Time
Content	10	10 minutes
Skills	10 or 15	10–15 minutes
Writing	1 prompt	10 minutes

Depending on the needs of your students, you may decide to administer the entire test in one sitting (about 30 minutes), or you may administer sections of the test in separate sittings.

To administer a test, give a copy of the test to each student. Have students write their names at the top of each page.

Directions for students appear at the top of each page. In this grade you may want to read the directions aloud as students read them silently. Then have students read the questions and mark or write their answers on the test pages.

For multiple-choice items, students fill in the circle before the correct answer to each item. For short-answer questions, students write a letter, a word, a phrase, or a sentence on the lines provided. For the Writing prompt, students write sentences or a paragraph on the lines provided.

During the administration, check to see that each student is following the directions, is answering the right items, and is marking responses correctly.

Administering Performance Assessments

In Part 4 of this manual, you will find a Performance Assessment for each unit in *People Together*. The **Performance Assessment** for each unit is one page intended for the teacher's use. It is based on the Unit Project, and it is designed to evaluate how well students can apply the content and skills taught in the unit.

The Unit Project and the Performance Assessment work in tandem to provide both instruction and assessment. When you have completed a unit, use the Performance Assessment to help prepare students to complete the Unit Project and then to evaluate their performance.

First, explain to students what they will be doing in the Unit Project.

Second, use the suggestions at the top of the Performance Assessment page to introduce the project and review instructional material from the unit.

Third, if appropriate for your students, explain what is expected of them and how their work will be evaluated through the Performance Assessment.

Scoring

The Unit Tests are designed to be scored by section (Content, Skills, Writing). For each Unit Test the correct responses are listed in the Answer Key (found in Part 2 of this manual).

For multiple-choice questions, the letter of the correct response is in the Answer Key. For short-answer items (such as fill-in-the-blank or matching), the correct letter, word, or phrase is listed in the Answer Key.

In some cases where questions require the students to supply their own answers in phrases or sentences, the Answer Key provides the expected response or the factual information required. However, the content and wording of the students' answers may vary from what is listed in the Answer Key. In these cases the Answer Key should be used only as a guideline for determining whether students' responses are correct or not.

Scoring the Unit Test: Content

To score the Content section, use the Answer Key to mark each answer correct or incorrect. There are ten items in this section. To determine a score for Content, add up the number of items answered correctly (for example, 7 of 10). To find the percentage score, multiply the number answered correctly by 10: 7 x 10 = 70%.

Scoring the Unit Test: Skills

To score the Skills section, use the Answer Key to mark each answer correct or incorrect. There are ten items in this section (except in Unit 3, which has 15 items). To determine a score for the Skills section, add up the number of items answered correctly (for example, 7 of 10). To find the percentage score for tests with ten items, multiply the number answered correctly by 10: 7 x 10 = 70%. To find the percentage score for a test with 15 items, divide the number answered correctly by the total number of items (for example, 12 ÷ 15 = .80, or 80%).

Scoring the Unit Test: Writing

To score the Writing section, use the Answer Key to evaluate each student's response. The Answer Key describes the characteristics of an *Excellent* response and an *Adequate* response. You may score the student's response as Excellent, Adequate, or Not Adequate based on the criteria listed in the Answer Key. Or, you may want to rate the student's response on a 4-point scale, as explained on the next page.

Passing Scores

The Unit Tests are based on the content and skills taught in the unit and are scored in relation to a criterion, or passing, score. In the Content and Skills sections, the recommended passing score is 70% (7 of 10 items answered correctly, or 11 of 15). For the Writing section, students should achieve a score of at least *adequate*, or at least 2 on the 4-point scale. (These are recommended passing scores; you may want to adjust them upward or downward for your students.)

Alternative Scoring Method for Writing: Using a 4-Point Scale

For the Writing section of the Unit Test, responses are intended to be scored as *Excellent, Adequate*, or *Not Adequate*. However, you may want to use an alternative method of scoring the student's response on a scale of 1–4 (or 0 for an unscorable response). Each response may be awarded zero to four points depending on its accuracy and completeness. For example, students who provide a partial response to an exercise might receive one point, while students who give a full and outstanding response would receive four points. (A student who does not respond to the exercise or whose response is for some reason unscorable would receive zero points.)

To score students' responses on a 4-point scale, use the rating scale defined below.

If you wish to convert a score on the 4-point scale to a percentage score, use this conversion chart.

Conversion Chart	
Number of Points	Percentage Score
1	25%
2	50%
3	75%
4	100%

4-Point Rating Scale

4 Excellent. The student makes an outstanding response that includes all or most of the elements listed in the Answer Key. This score indicates that the student not only understands the necessary information and concepts but also exhibits additional insight into their meaning and importance.

3 Good. The student makes an above-average response that includes many of the elements listed in the Answer Key for both an adequate and an excellent response, indicating that the student has a firm grasp of the necessary concepts and information.

2 Fair. The student makes a satisfactory response that includes the elements listed in the Answer Key for an adequate response, indicating that the student has satisfactory knowledge and understanding of the necessary concepts and information.

1 Poor. The student makes a minimal response that does not include the elements listed in the Answer Key for an adequate response, indicating that the student has not learned or does not understand the necessary concepts and information.

0 No Response. The student did not respond to the exercise, or the response is illegible or for some other reason unscorable.

Scoring Performance Assessments

Each Performance Assessment includes a scoring rubric designed to help you evaluate each student's performance. The rubric describes the characteristics of the project on a 4-point scale: Excellent, Good, Fair, Poor (or Unscorable). Use the scoring rubric to score each student's work as a 4, 3, 2, 1, or 0.

If you wish to convert a score on the 4-point scale to a percentage score, use the conversion chart on page T7.

Portfolio Assessment Opportunities

The Unit Projects are ideal activities for self-assessment, peer assessment, and inclusion in a portfolio. The "Portfolio Opportunity" guidelines suggest ways to engage students in evaluating their own work through self-assessment or peer assessment before displaying their work or placing it in their portfolios.

Self-Assessment and Peer Assessment

Students can learn a great deal from understanding and applying the standards of good work to their own achievements. In using the Performance Assessments, encourage students to assess their own work by pointing out what they think is good about it and what they think they might do better next time. You might want to have them complete the Self-Assessment Checklist on page T9 after they have completed a Unit Project (or other type of project activity).

When students have become familiar with self-assessment, have them practice peer assessment by working with partners. Encourage students to assess the work of others by pointing out positive aspects of it and discussing what they think is good about the other student's work. You may want to model this process for students

so they understand the positive tone that should be applied. You might want to have them complete the Peer Assessment Checklist on page T10 to assess a student's work, a partner's work, or a group's work on a Unit Project or other activity.

Group Assessment

In many projects and activities, students will be working with partners or in groups. To assess an individual's performance in a group situation, you can gather information through observation of the students as they work, through conferences with students in which they discuss their work, through self-assessments, and through peer assessments. You may want to use the Group Assessment Chart on page T11 to help evaluate and record individual performances.

Class Summary Chart

To develop a profile of student performance on the assessments for each unit, you may want to record the Unit Test and Performance Assessment scores on the Class Summary Chart on page T12. From the student's Unit Test scores and Performance Assessment results, you can determine an overall rating of the student's performance for each unit. This overall rating may be expressed on the 4-point scale, as a percentage score, or as a letter grade.

Self-Assessment Checklist

Name _____ **Date** _____

Unit Project _____

1. What did you do in this project?

_____

_ _

_____

2. What did you do well?

_____

_ _

_____

3. What parts of the project could you do better next time?

_____

_ _

_____

4. What did you learn from this project?

_____

_ _

_____

5. What did you like best about this project?

_____

_ _

_____

Peer Assessment Checklist

Name _____ **Date** _____

Project or Activity _____

1. What did your classmate do in this project?

_____

- - - - - - - - - - - - - - - - - - - -

_____

_____

- - - - - - - - - - - - - - - - - - - -

_____

2. What was the best thing your classmate did?

_____

- - - - - - - - - - - - - - - - - - - -

_____

_____

- - - - - - - - - - - - - - - - - - - -

_____

3. How would you rate your classmate's work? (Circle one)

Excellent   Good   Fair   Needs Improvement

4. What suggestions would you make to help your classmate do better next time?

_____

- - - - - - - - - - - - - - - - - - - -

_____

_____

- - - - - - - - - - - - - - - - - - - -

_____

Group Assessment Chart

Class _____ Project or Activity _____

Directions. Rate each individual's performance as 4, 3, 2, 1, or 0 on each of the criteria listed below. (4 = Excellent, 3 = Good, 2 = Fair, 1 = Poor, 0 = Unscorable)

Student Names																						
Criteria																						
Participates in group work																						
Contributes to project success																						
Listens to others																						
Asks and answers questions																						
Stays on task																						
Cooperates with others																						
Offers positive suggestions																						
Exhibits leadership																						
Compliments and encourages others																						
Overall Rating																						

CLASS SUMMARY CHART

Class _____ Unit _____

Student Name	Unit Test: Content	Unit Test: Skills	Unit Test: Writing	Performance Assessment	Overall Rating

Part 2

Answer Key

Contents

ANSWER KEY

Content

1. b
2. a
3. c
4. a
5. c

6. group
7. rules
8. community
9. neighbors
10. citizen

Skills

1–2. Any two: The house, tree, and hill are the same, in both pictures the girl has dark hair.

3–5. Any three: The girl is older; her hair is longer; the dog is bigger; the car is different.

6. 28

7. Thursday
8. Tuesday
9. February 12
10. February 20

Writing

An adequate response will mention two rules, such as "No TV" and "Wash your hands before dinner." An excellent response will state two rules that are relevant to a guest. Examples: No TV on weeknights; wash your hands before eating; say "please" and "thank you."

ANSWER KEY

Content

1. a
2. b
3. c
4. a
5. c

6. ocean
7. valley
8. river
9. mountain
10. continent

Skills

1. west
2. north
3. north
4. south
5. east

6. three
7. plains
8. hills
9. hills
10. west

Writing

An adequate response will state the direction of two trips correctly. An excellent response will state the direction of all three trips correctly. The family will travel west to Rapid City, north to Selby, and east to Miller.

Content

1. b
2. a
3. c
4. b
5. a

6. service
7. shelter
8. wants
9. transportation
10. needs

Skills

1. A farmer grew and picked the peanuts.
2. to the factory
3. They are put into cans.
4. at the store or market
5. They'll put the peanuts on the shelves; people will buy the peanuts.
6. the post office

7. Pine Street
8. Connie
9. Pine Street and Maple Lane
10. Salem Road to Maple Lane
11–12. Things That Grow: Carrots, Tree
13–15. Things That Are Made: Chair, Shoes, Book

Writing

An adequate response will describe one person who makes goods and one person who provides a service. Example: baker, doctor. An excellent response will explain what each person provides. Example: A baker makes bread. A doctor takes care of you when you are sick.

Content

1. b
2. a
3. c
4. b
5. a

6. petition
7. tax
8. flag
9. city council
10. vote

Skills

1. Mom and Penny wait for the train.
2. Train comes into station.
3. Mom and Penny get on the train.
4. They walked (or rode) to the train station, or they packed their suitcases.
5. by time

6. Drew a picture.
7. Wednesday
8. Thursday
9. Cut paper.
10. Put flag on house.

Writing

An adequate response will state that the stars represent the 50 current states and the stripes represent the 13 original states. It will also say how we can honor our flag and our country by saying the Pledge of Allegiance. An excellent response will add how the pledge is said at the start of the day in the classroom.

ANSWER KEY

Content

1. c
2. a
3. b
4. c
5. b
6. Vikings
7. Christopher Columbus
8. Timucua
9. Powhatan
10. Harriet Tubman

Skills

1. C4
2. A1
3. A4
4. zoo
5. A2
6. You can learn about your family's history.
7. ways to learn about your family's history
8. The Tsimshian made many things out of wood.
9. things that the Tsimshian made from wood
10. Many pioneers moved to the West.

Writing

An adequate response will state that the colonists came from Europe and that St. Augustine was built first. An excellent response will add that St. Augustine was Spanish, and Jamestown and Plymouth were English.

ANSWER KEY

Content

1. c
2. b
3. a
4. b
5. a
6. Statue of Liberty
7. The Alamo
8. Gateway Arch
9. Golden Gate Bridge
10. Grand Canyon

Skills

1. Sam Houston became governor.
2. Houston wanted to be the governor of Texas. When Texas became a state, Houston ran for governor.
3–5. Any three: She traveled to Europe. She studied buildings in Europe. She became an architect. She planned buildings.

6. 2
7. Maya Lin
8. 4
9. George Washington
10. 3

Writing

An adequate response will state that Independence Day is important because it honors our country's birthday or the day our country became the United States of America. The response should also describe at least one way Independence Day is celebrated. An excellent response will further explain that this holiday reminds us that the Declaration of Independence was signed on July 4, 1776.

Part 3

Unit Tests

CONTENT

Fill in the circle before the correct answer.

1. What kind of community is just outside a city?
   - ⓐ rural area   ⓑ suburb   ⓒ urban area

2. Places with farms and open countryside are called ____.
   - ⓐ rural areas   ⓑ suburbs   ⓒ urban areas

3. What is the name for a city and the places around it?
   - ⓐ rural area   ⓑ suburb   ⓒ urban area

4. People who live far away from each other can keep in touch by ____.
   - ⓐ talking on the telephone
   - ⓑ playing baseball
   - ⓒ meeting at a park

5. What is something that good citizens do?
   - ⓐ break the rules
   - ⓑ throw things on the street
   - ⓒ work together to solve problems

CONTENT

Choose the word each sentence tells about. Write the word on the line.

neighbors	group	citizen
rules	community	

6. This can be a team or the people in a class.

_____

7. These tell us what to do and what not to do.

_____

8. This has many different neighborhoods.

_____

9. These are the people who live near you.

_____

10. This is what a member of a country, state, or community is called.

_____

SKILLS

Look at the pictures of Tina. Then answer the questions.

Tina, age 3

Tina, age 7

Write two things that are **alike** in the two pictures.

1. _____

2. _____

Write three things that are **different** in the two pictures.

3. _____

4. _____

5. _____

SKILLS

Use the calendar to answer the questions.

FEBRUARY						
Sunday	Monday	Tuesday	Wednesday	Thursday	Friday	Saturday
			1	2 Groundhog Day	3	4
5	6	7	8	9	10	11
12	13	14 Valentine's Day	15	16	17	18
19	20 Presidents' Day	21	22	23	24	25
26	27	28				

6. How many days are in February?

_____

7. What day of the week is February 9?

_____

8. What day of the week is Valentine's Day?

_____

9. What is the date of the second Sunday in February?

_____

10. When is Presidents' Day?

_____

WRITING

Look at this picture.

Now think about the rules at your home. Write two rules that a friend who visits your house should know.

Rule I
_____

- -
_____

Rule 2
_____

- -
_____

CONTENT

Fill in the circle before the correct answer.

1. A _____ is where the leaders of a state work.

   ⓐ capital   ⓑ shelter   ⓒ continent

2. The name of the continent we live on is _____.

   ⓐ Mexico   ⓑ North America   ⓒ Canada

3. The United States is the name of the _____ where we live.

   ⓐ community   ⓑ state   ⓒ country

4. The country to the north of the United States is _____.

   ⓐ Canada   ⓑ Texas   ⓒ Mexico

5. Air, water, and trees are all _____.

   ⓐ shelters   ⓑ plants   ⓒ natural resources

CONTENT

Write the word from the box that goes with each clue.

mountain	continent	valley
river	ocean	

6. a very large body of
   salt water

   _____

7. low land between hills
   or mountains

   _____

8. a long body of water that
   flows across the land

   _____

9. the highest kind of
   land

   _____

10. a very large body of
    land

   _____

SKILLS

Use the map and the compass rose to answer the questions.

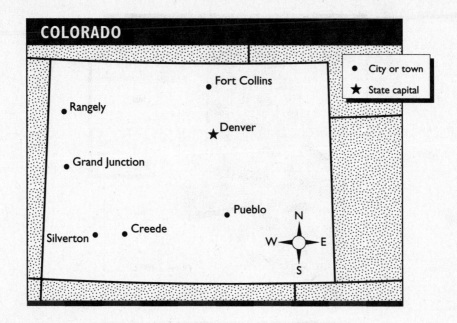

1. Mike lives in Denver. He goes to Grand Junction. In which direction does he travel?

_____
_ _ _ _ _ _ _ _ _ _ _ _ _
_____

2. In what part of the state is Fort Collins?

_____
_ _ _ _ _ _ _ _ _ _ _ _ _
_____

3. Tina lives in Grand Junction. She goes to Rangely. In which direction does she travel?

_____
_ _ _ _ _ _ _ _ _ _ _ _ _
_____

4. Is Pueblo north or south of Denver?

_____
_ _ _ _ _ _ _ _ _ _ _ _ _
_____

5. Is Creede east or west of Silverton?

_____
_ _ _ _ _ _ _ _ _ _ _ _ _

SKILLS

Use the map to answer the questions.

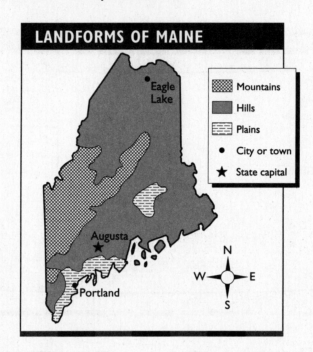

LANDFORMS OF MAINE

Eagle Lake

Augusta

Portland

Mountains
Hills
Plains
● City or town
★ State capital

N
W ● E
S

6. How many kinds of landforms are shown on the map?

_____

_____

_____

7. On what kind of land is Portland?

_____

_____

_____

8. On what kind of land is the state capital?

_____

_____

_____

9. On what kind of land is Eagle Lake?

_____

_____

_____

10. In what part of the state are mountains?

_____

_____

WRITING

Sam lives in Pierre, South Dakota. This summer Sam's family will make three car trips to visit friends who live in the other towns you see on this map.

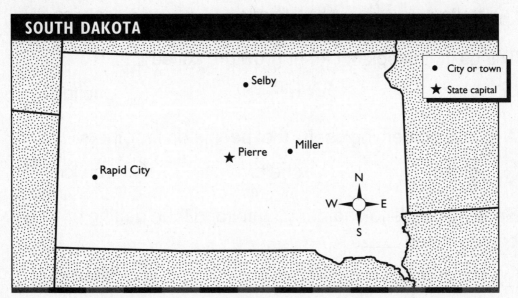

Write a sentence about each trip Sam's family will take. Tell in what direction they will drive from Pierre to each town.

_____
- -
_____
- -
_____
- -
_____
- -
_____

CONTENT

Fill in the circle before the correct answer.

1. A _____ is a building where things are made.
   - (a) route
   - (b) factory
   - (c) service

2. Things that people make or grow are called _____.
   - (a) goods
   - (b) rules
   - (c) capitals

3. A _____ is something useful that people do for others.
   - (a) market
   - (b) shelter
   - (c) service

4. Sending goods to another country and then getting other goods back is called _____.
   - (a) transportation
   - (b) trade
   - (c) shelter

5. People work at jobs to _____.
   - (a) earn money
   - (b) join groups
   - (c) follow rules

CONTENT

Draw a line from the picture to the word that tells about it.

6.    wants

7. 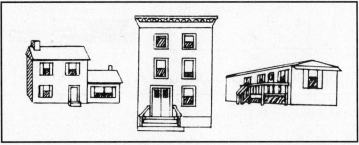   service

8.    needs

9. 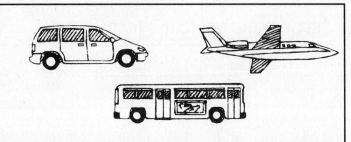   shelter

10. 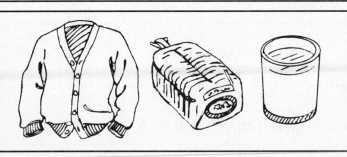   transportation

SKILLS

This flow chart shows how peanuts get from the farm to a store.

A    B    C

I. What do you think happened before picture A?

_____

_____

2. Where is the farmer taking the peanuts?

_____

_____

3. What happens after the peanuts get to the factory?

_____

_____

4. Where do people buy peanuts?

_____

_____

5. What do you think will happen after picture C?

_____

_____

SKILLS

This map shows the route of the school bus from the school to Joe's house. Use the map to answer the questions.

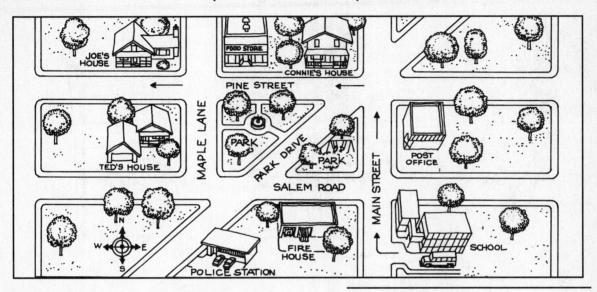

6. What building does the bus go by on Main Street?

   _____
   _____

7. From Main Street the bus turns left onto _____.

   _____
   _____

8. Joe, Connie, and Ted take the school bus home. Who gets off the bus first?

   _____
   _____

9. Joe lives at the corner of which two streets?

   _____
   _____

10. The bus could go a different way from Main Street to Joe's house. Tell how the bus could go.

   _____
   _____
   _____

SKILLS

Look at the pictures. Sort them into groups. Write the name of each picture in the group where it belongs.

carrots

tree

chair

book

shoes

THINGS THAT GROW	THINGS THAT ARE MADE
_____	_____
11. _____	13. _____
_____	_____
12. _____	14. _____
	_____
	15. _____

Macmillan/McGraw-Hill

WRITING

Look at the pictures of people doing their jobs. Some are making or growing **goods**. Others are doing **services**. Think about the people who work in your community. Write a sentence about someone who makes goods. Write a sentence about someone who does a service.

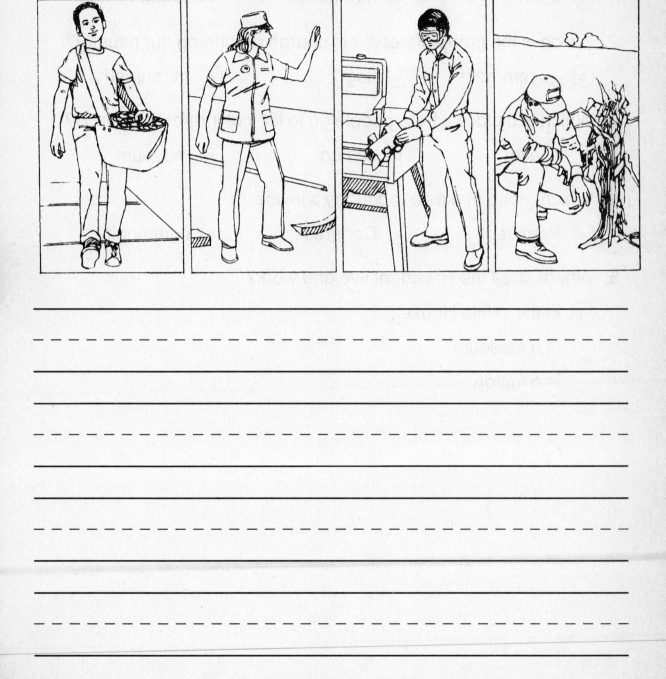

_____

- -

_____

- -

_____

- -

_____

- -

_____

CONTENT

Fill in the circle before the correct answer.

1. What kind of building honors a person or something that happened?

   (a) factory   (b) monument   (c) White House

2. Which is the group of people in charge of running our country?

   (a) government   (b) flag   (c) monuments

3. Which is a place where people go to look at interesting things?

   (a) shelter   (b) symbol   (c) museum

4. Which group makes our country's laws?

   (a) President   (b) Congress   (c) community

5. Where does the President live and work?

   (a) in the White House

   (b) in a museum

   (c) in a factory

CONTENT

Write the word or words from the box that best fit in each sentence.

| city council | petition | vote | tax | flag |

_____

6. A ____ is a special letter that many people sign.

- - - - - - - - - - - - - - -

_____

7. Money that people pay to a community is called a ____.

- - - - - - - - - - - - - - -

_____

8. The ____ is a symbol for our country.

- - - - - - - - - - - - - - -

_____

9. The ____ is a group of people that run a city.

- - - - - - - - - - - - - - -

_____

10. People ____ to choose or decide something.

- - - - - - - - - - - - - - -

_____

SKILLS

Look at the pictures. Mom and Penny are going on a trip. Think about how to put the pictures in order. Then write a sentence to answer each question.

I. What happens first?

_____

- -

_____

2. What happens next?

_____

- -

_____

3. What happens last?

_____

- -

_____

4. What do you think Mom and Penny did before they waited for the train?

_____

- -

_____

5. How did you put these pictures in order?

_____

- -

_____

SKILLS

Frank Duck made a flag for his family's house. The time line shows what he did each day. Use the time line to answer the questions.

Monday	Tuesday	Wednesday	Thursday	Friday
Drew a picture.	Cut paper.	Pasted flag together.	Colored flag.	Put flag on house.

6. What did Frank do first?

_____

7. On what day did Frank paste the flag together?

_____

8. On what day did Frank color the flag?

_____

9. What did Frank do on Tuesday?

_____

10. What did Frank do on the last day?

_____

WRITING

Look at the picture of our country's flag.

Tell what the stars and stripes are symbols for. Then tell how people can honor the flag.

- -

- -

- -

- -

- -

CONTENT

Fill in the circle before the correct answer.

1. The first people to live in America were ____.

   ⓐ Pilgrims   ⓑ colonists   ⓒ Native Americans

2. Many years later, explorers came from Europe. They hoped to find ____.

   ⓐ gold   ⓑ food   ⓒ houses

3. People from Europe came to live in places like Jamestown and St. Augustine. These people were called ____.

   ⓐ leaders   ⓑ colonists   ⓒ Native Americans

4. When one person owns another, it is called ____.

   ⓐ history   ⓑ independence   ⓒ slavery

5. Over the years the United States became crowded, so some people moved to the West. Others moved north. These people were called ____.

   ⓐ citizens   ⓑ pioneers   ⓒ slaves

CONTENT

Read each sentence. Draw a line from the sentence to the
name that it tells about.

6. They were among the first   Vikings
   explorers from Europe to come
   to America.

7. He sailed from Spain in   Harriet Tubman
   1492.

8. These Native Americans   Powhatan
   lived near St. Augustine.

9. These Native Americans   Christopher Columbus
   helped the colonists at
   Jamestown.

10. She helped people to   Timucua
    escape from slavery.

Name: _____   Date: _____

SKILLS

Use the grid map to answer the questions.

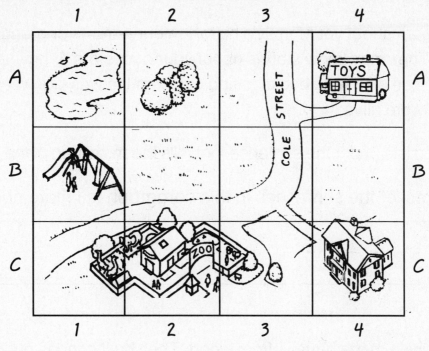

1. There is a house in which square? _____

   _____

2. In which square is the pond? _____

   _____

3. The toy store is in which square? _____

   _____

4. What is in C2? _____

   _____

5. Where are the trees? _____

SKILLS

Read each paragraph. Then answer the questions.

You can learn about your family's history. Your parents or grandparents can help. They may know stories about your ancestors or have pictures of them. You can also read books to find out what life was like when your ancestors were alive.

6. Draw a line under the sentence that tells the main idea of the paragraph.

7. The rest of the sentences in this paragraph tell more about

_____

— —

_____ .

The Tsimshian made houses from wood. They built canoes out of wood. They also used wood to make totem poles. The Tsimshian made many things out of wood.

8. Draw a line under the sentence that tells the main idea of the paragraph.

9. The rest of the sentences in this paragraph tell more about

_____

— —

_____ .

Many pioneers moved to the West. First they traveled to Missouri. Then they rode in wagons to California and Oregon. When they got to the West, the pioneers made new homes.

10. Draw a line under the sentence that tells the main idea of the paragraph.

WRITING

This map shows some places built by colonists in America.

PLACES BUILT BY COLONISTS

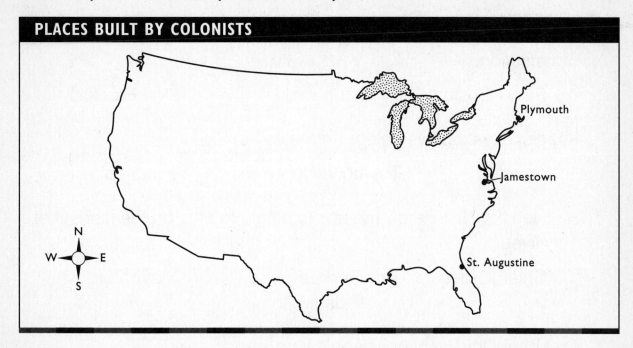

Write two sentences. First tell where the people who lived in these places came from. Then tell which place was built first.

_____

- -

_____

_____

- -

_____

_____

- -

_____

_____

- -

_____

CONTENT

Fill in the circle before the correct answer.

1. _____ was a scientist and an inventor. He also helped to write the Constitution.

   ⓐ Sam Houston   ⓑ Abraham Lincoln   ⓒ Ben Franklin

2. Special days that we celebrate are called _____.

   ⓐ parades   ⓑ holidays   ⓒ customs

3. _____ led the Nez Percé Indians in a fight to stay on the land where they lived.

   ⓐ Chief Joseph   ⓑ George Washington   ⓒ Maya Lin

4. On Labor Day we honor people who _____.

   ⓐ play   ⓑ work   ⓒ travel

5. _____ was once a slave. She helped people escape from slavery.

   ⓐ Sojourner Truth   ⓑ Clara Barton   ⓒ Maya Lin

CONTENT

Read each description. Draw a line from the description to the name that it matches best.

6. This is a symbol of freedom. It stands for people who came to our country looking for better lives.

Grand Canyon

7. This is a fort in Texas. It is the place where people from Texas fought to be free from Mexico.

Gateway Arch

8. This place in St. Louis, Missouri, helps us remember the pioneers.

Statue of Liberty

9. This place is a "gate" to the city of San Francisco.

Golden Gate Bridge

10. This place is in Arizona. It is very deep.

The Alamo

SKILLS

Read each paragraph. Then answer the questions about making predictions.

Texas won its independence in 1836. Sam Houston was its first leader. He worked hard to help Texas become a state. Houston wanted to be the governor of Texas. When Texas became a state, Houston ran for governor.

1. What do you think Sam Houston did next?

   _____

   _____

   _____

2. Draw a line under two sentences that give clues to what happened next.

Maya Lin grew up in Ohio. She worked hard in school. She read many books and studied buildings. She learned to draw. Then she wanted to travel to Europe. She wanted to see the buildings in Europe. Maya Lin hoped to become an architect—a person who plans buildings.

Write three predictions about what Maya Lin did when she got older.

3. _____

   _____

4. _____

   _____

5. _____

SKILLS

At the library Carl found books about some special Americans. The bar graph shows how many books he found. Use the bar graph to answer the questions.

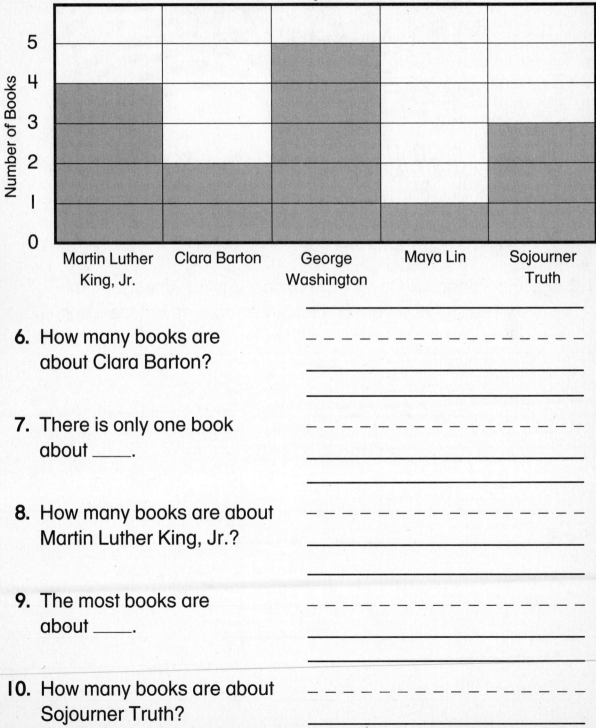

Books About Special Americans

6. How many books are about Clara Barton?

7. There is only one book about _____.

8. How many books are about Martin Luther King, Jr.?

9. The most books are about _____.

10. How many books are about Sojourner Truth?

WRITING

Look at the picture. It shows some of the ways a community celebrates Independence Day.

Tell why Independence Day is an important day for Americans to remember. Then tell how your community celebrates Independence Day.

_____

- -

_____

- -

_____

_____

- -

_____

- -

Part 4

Performance Assessments

Contents

Performance Assessments

Unit 1 Project: Make a Helping Hands Puppet

Goal
The child will identify a person who helps him or her and what the person does to help.

Suggestions:
1. Have children review the unit to find pictures of people who help, or have them brainstorm a list of people they see often and discuss what some of these people do.
2. To model the process, give an example of someone, such as a spouse or colleague, who helps you, describe some of the things the person does, and make a puppet of your own.

Portfolio Opportunities
Have children evaluate their puppets by telling you what is good about them. Then have children display their puppets in the classroom or place them in their portfolios.

SCORING RUBRIC

4 An **excellent** puppet has a paper hand glued onto a craft stick. It includes the child's name, a picture of a person who helps (such as a parent or grandparent, teacher, brother or sister, bus driver), and five things that the person does to help the child. Helpful things the person does should be described in words or phrases (on the fingers of the hand) written with correct spelling, for example: Mother makes meals, helps me get dressed, takes care of me, drives me to school, reads to me.

3 A **good** puppet includes the child's name, a picture of a person who helps, and four things that the person does to help the child. These things are described in words or phrases written with generally correct spelling.

2 A **fair** puppet includes a picture or the name of a person who helps and three things that the person does to help the child. It may also include things that the person does that do not directly help the child. Words and phrases are written with recognizable spelling.

1 A **poor** puppet includes a picture or the name of a person who helps and only one or two things that the person does to help the child, or it may include things that the person does that do not directly help the child. Words and phrases may not use recognizable spelling.

0 An **unscorable** puppet does not include a picture of a person or things that the person does to help the child, or it has words that are not readable.

Performance Assessments

Unit 2 Project: Make Up a New Continent

Goal

The child will demonstrate an understanding of continents and landforms.

Suggestions:

1. Have children look through the unit to review continents and landforms, and ask children to name landforms in the local community or in other areas they know about.

2. To model the process, use a globe or a physical map of the world to identify continents and landforms. Then invent a continent of your own and describe what it is like.

Portfolio Opportunities

Have children exchange their works with partners. Have the partner evaluate the child's work by telling something he or she likes about it. The partner might write a sentence on the bottom of the paper describing what he or she likes. Then have children display their works on a wall or a bulletin board or place them in their portfolios.

SCORING RUBRIC

4 An **excellent** project shows a large body of land labeled with a made-up name suitable for a continent. The name is written with recognizable spelling and correct capitalization. The body of land is surrounded by ocean on at least three sides and has at least three different landforms shown (mountains, hills, plains, valleys, peninsulas, islands). Different landforms are presented with different colors and are recognizable to a partner as different landforms.

3 A **good** project shows a large body of land labeled with a made-up name suitable for a continent. The name is written with recognizable spelling and may use correct capitalization. The body of land is surrounded by ocean on at least three sides and has at least two different landforms shown. Different landforms are presented with different colors and are recognizable to a partner as different landforms.

2 A **fair** project shows a large body of land labeled with a made-up name, written with recognizable spelling. The continent has at least two different landforms or bodies of water (oceans, rivers, lakes) shown. Different landforms are presented with different colors and are recognizable to a partner as different landforms.

1 A **poor** project shows a body of land labeled with a name that is not made-up or is not suitable for a continent. It has only one landform or body of water shown, or none. Landforms are not recognizable to a partner.

0 An **unscorable** project does not show a large body of land or any landforms, or it is not recognizable as a continent.

Performance Assessments

Unit 3 Project: Selling Goods or Services

Goal

The child will identify goods or services appropriate for a store.

Suggestions:

1. Have children brainstorm a list of common goods and services, or ask children to describe the kinds of stores they have been to and what is sold there.
2. To model the process, use a local store, a mail order catalogue, or a newspaper advertising supplement as an example to talk about goods and services sold in stores.

Portfolio Opportunities

Discuss the project with each child and have him or her describe the kind of store shown in the model and the goods or services available. Have the child complete a self-assessment checklist after your discussion. Encourage children to display their stores in a designated area in the classroom, and have them place their self-assessments in their portfolios.

SCORING RUBRIC
4 An **excellent** model shows the inside of a store glued into a shoe box. The store has a sign with an appropriate name, which uses correct capitalization and spelling, and it shows five or more different goods or services appropriate to the type of store (for example, a grocery store, drugstore, hardware store, clothing store, or department store). Certain types of stores may show both goods and services; for example, a hair salon may show hairstyling and shampooing (services), and hair-care products displayed on a shelf (goods). If prompted, the child can distinguish between goods and services.
3 A **good** model shows the inside of a store glued into a shoe box. The store has a sign with an appropriate name, written with generally correct capitalization and spelling, and it shows three or four different goods or services appropriate to the type of store.
2 A **fair** model shows the inside of a store glued into a shoe box. The store has a sign with a name, written with recognizable spelling, and it shows at least two different goods or services appropriate to the type of store. It may also include goods or services that are not appropriate to the type of store (such as a pair of shoes in a grocery store), or it may include some examples that are not goods or services (such as pictures of customers or shopping carts).
1 A **poor** model shows the inside of a store, but the store does not have a sign with an appropriate name, and it shows only one or no goods or services appropriate to the type of store. It may include examples of things that are not goods or services.
0 An **unscorable** model does not include examples of goods or services or is not recognizable as a store.

Performance Assessments

Unit 4 Project: Make a Washington, D.C., Cup

Goal

The child will identify a favorite monument or building in Washington, D.C., and find one fact about it.

Suggestions:

1. Have children review the unit to identify a favorite building or monument in Washington, D.C., and discuss ways to find information about it; for example, using an almanac, obtaining brochures or guide books from a travel agent or the library, or asking a parent for help.
2. To model the process, describe your own favorite monument or building in Washington, D.C., and give one fact about it that children would not know.

Portfolio Opportunities

Have children exchange cups with partners. Ask the partner to evaluate the child's work and complete a peer assessment checklist. Then have children display their cups in the classroom and place the peer assessments in their portfolios.

SCORING RUBRIC

4 An **excellent** cup shows a picture of a monument or building in Washington, D.C. (for example, the Washington Monument, Lincoln Memorial, Capitol, White House), and one fact about it that the child would not have known from the unit. The picture is on one side of the cup, and the fact is stated on the other side, written with correct use of grammar, punctuation, capitalization, and spelling (for example: The Washington Monument was completed in 1884).

3 A **good** cup shows a picture of a monument or building in Washington, D.C., and one fact about it. The fact is taken from the unit. It is written with generally correct use of grammar, punctuation, capitalization, and spelling (for example: This monument was named for George Washington).

2 A **fair** cup shows a picture of a monument or building in Washington, D.C., and one fact about it. Facts may include some errors in grammar, punctuation, capitalization, and spelling.

1 A **poor** cup shows the name or a picture of a monument or building in Washington, D.C., but does not include a fact about it.

0 An **unscorable** cup does not include a recognizable picture of a monument or a building and does not include a fact about it, or the fact is unreadable.

Performance Assessments

Unit 5 Project: Make a Picture Time Line

Goal
The child will identify things that happened in the unit and demonstrate a sense of historical sequence.

Suggestions:
1. Have children review the unit to identify things that happened, and discuss the historical sequence by asking questions, such as: Which people were here first? Which group came from Europe to America first?
2. To model the process of making a time line, draw pictures on the chalkboard and have children identify the sequence, or show an example of a time line, such as a chronological listing of TV shows.

Portfolio Opportunities
Have children evaluate their works by discussing them with their partners, telling what they think is good about them and what they think was hard about this project. Then have children display their picture time lines or place them in their portfolios.

SCORING RUBRIC

4 An **excellent** time line shows pictures of three things that happened in the unit presented in correct historical sequence. Each picture is labeled correctly and includes a sentence describing the thing. Labels and sentences are written with correct use of grammar, punctuation, capitalization, and spelling (for example, "Explorers came from Europe to America").

3 A **good** time line shows pictures of three things from the unit presented in correct historical sequence. Each picture is labeled correctly with a descriptive sentence. Sentences are written with generally correct punctuation, capitalization, and spelling.

2 A **fair** time line shows pictures of three things from the unit. The things may be presented in a somewhat confused sequence, or they may be somewhat indistinct. Each picture is labeled with a descriptive name or phrase. Labels may include errors in capitalization and spelling.

1 A **poor** time line may show pictures of three things, but they are not distinctly different; the things are presented out of sequence; or there is no description of each thing.

0 An **unscorable** time line does not include three different things, is not presented in a sequence, or does not have recognizable labels.

Performance Assessments

Unit 6 Project: Make a Holiday Calendar

Goal

The child will make a calendar showing a favorite holiday.

Suggestions:

1. Show children the calendar for the current month and discuss the holiday(s) in the month, or ask children to name their favorite holidays and describe some things associated with the holiday.
2. Model the process by discussing your favorite holiday, in what month it occurs, and what kinds of things you associate with the holiday.

Portfolio Opportunities

Discuss the project with each child and have the child describe her or his calendar. Then have the child complete a self-assessment checklist after your discussion. Encourage children to display their calendars, and have them place their self-assessments in their portfolios.

SCORING RUBRIC

4 An **excellent** calendar shows the name of the month written at the top. It includes the correct number of days and a number in each box. It has the name of a holiday written in the correct box, and it includes five or more pictures of things associated with the holiday. Names are written with correct capitalization and spelling.

3 A **good** calendar shows the name of the month written at the top. It includes a number in each box, although the number of days in the month may not be correct. It has the name of a holiday written in the correct box, and it includes four or more pictures of things associated with the holiday. Names are written with generally correct capitalization and spelling.

2 A **fair** calendar shows the name of the month written at the top. It includes a number in each box, although the number of days in the month may not be correct. It has the name of a holiday, although it may not be written in the correct box, and it includes two or three pictures of things associated with the holiday. Names may include some errors in capitalization or spelling.

1 A **poor** calendar does not include the name of the month, or it is written incorrectly. It may include numbers in the boxes, but the number of days in the month or the sequence of numbers is incorrect. It has the name of a holiday, but it is written in an incorrect box or is not in the month shown. It may have one or two pictures of things associated with the holiday.

0 An **unscorable** calendar does not include a recognizable name or a holiday, and there are no recognizable dates.